Manners in the Digital Age

The Technology Etiquette Handbook for Corporate America

Christine Mansfield

No part of this publication may be reproduced, stored or transmitted in any form or by any means, mechanical, photocopying, scanning or otherwise imaged, as permitted under Section 107 or 108 of the United States Copyright Act, without the prior written permission of the author.

Limit of Liability/ Disclaimer of Warranty: While the author have used best efforts to prepare this book, there is no representation or warranty to the accuracy or completeness of the book's contents. The author is not liable for any loss of profit or any other commercial damages, including but not limited to special, incidental, consequential or other damages.

Readers should be aware that online site references our sources offered as citations may change or not be maintained since the time of publication or reading.

2014 © All Rights Reserved.

Table of Contents

CHAPTER I 3

Background/ Overview 3

    Communication..5

    The Foundation of Technology Etiquette 8

CHAPTER II 10

Messaging Etiquette 10

    Email - Overview 11

    Email Responsiveness 11

        Best Practices: Email Content..11

        Best Practices: Email Addressing – a Lost Art?..............................13

    Design options: 15

    File Attachment protocols: 17

    Best practices for File Attachments: 20

    Signatures 21

    Using Text Messaging 22

    Best Practices for Text Messaging and Social App:..............................22

CHAPTER III 23

Social Media...23

    Social Media & Etiquette 24

CHAPTER IV 29

Remote Conferencing 29

    Conferencing Checklist 33

CHAPTER V 34

Compliance 34

    Compliance & Policy 35

CHAPTER I

Background/ Overview

In any office or public gathering, one glaring observation can be made. Head down, at least one person's eyes fixate to a screen. Ringtones and notifications compete with face to face interactions. The omnipresence of "in-hand" devices challenges the most seasoned communicators' etiquette in daily conversation. From ringtone interruptions to Facebook posts, employees harbor varying practices in the use and access of smartphones, tablets and laptops in the presence of others, or professional standards for online channels. Employers traditionally lack a policy to govern technology etiquette as other communication channels. Our technology training offers best practices in email, texting, social media, conferencing and file distribution etiquette. This book creates a framework of expectations to set between employer and employees for technology manners. This book also outlines the publicity, branding, legal and compliance considerations for policy making. Our best practices foster a balance between the efficiency, marketing and socialization benefits of technology, while safeguarding the corporate culture, its intelligence and its brand.

Despite technology's explosive growth, etiquette often lacks a clear definition in the digitized workplace. Instruction manuals exist to explain hardware and software use or define telephone answering procedures, letterhead use and brand logo representation in print and oral communications. But companies fail to address etiquette and usage for the fastest growing, most potentially damaging technology channels of messaging, email, remote conferencing or social media. Employees lack a comprehensive plan or procedure on device usage and management as a communication tool. The missing chapter eludes many companies: the "etiquette" instruction manual to best use this technology. How should an employee, a supervisor, a manager or an executive manage this increasing technology dependence on 24x7 communications, but maintain a professional level of decorum and respect? Without a baseline standard, corporations lack documentation or enforcement in behavior lapses, mediating complaints, enforcing discipline or defending litigation.

Challenges emerge to integrate technology within the corporate culture, without compromising efficiencies, relationships and communication already in place. Establishing a protocol is step one to enforce technology usage consistent with the brand, mission and other communication channels. By standardizing technology etiquette and training, the corporation sustains a level of professionalism and communication standards consistent with all other channels and brand representation. It's time for *Manners in the digital age*: accessible, professional, 24x7 and defined.

The ubiquity of voicemail, email or conferencing tools lends a false sense of assumed policy or proper use. Without training or guidance, users interpret policy and appropriate use differently. Employees' subjective interpretations differ across departments, locations, levels and individuals. Varying etiquette practices result in inconsistent uses of technology and often cause disruption, tension or morale issues. Our shared best practices establish clear expectations and consistent standards for email and text messaging, audio and video conferencing and social media use. Whether lunchroom tweets or meeting texts, employers can gain valuable best practices from this book on where, when and how to respectfully balance technology use with etiquette. With mixed demographics in an office, the corporate morale can improve with an etiquette standard defined across offline, electronic and online channels for all employees to follow.

We recommend that each organization establish a professional code of conduct for technology use and include social media. Etiquette policies define a best practice and foster a more compliant use of technology for all employees. The technology team or the marketing department should not be the only beneficiary of technology etiquette training. With the omnipresence of Internet enabled devices, all employees benefit from training. Our best practices find an etiquette policy and training improve employee understanding and reduce the number of infractions. Policy documentation ultimately reduces human resource claims, liability and litigation risks. (Flynn, 1998)

Communication

Communication, regardless of the medium, is one of the most important relationship tools in business. The dictionary defines communication as the imparting or exchange of information, ideas or feelings. (Edition, 2009) Its etymologic root derives from the fourteenth century, Old French word communicacion and the Latin word communication, or "to share, divide out; import, inform; join, unite, participate in." (Online Etymology Dictionary - Communication, 2013) Fast forward to the modern era, many communication channels now exchange information in non-verbal, verbal, printed, viral, email, social, multi-media, graphic and online channels. The ability to communicate encompasses a dizzying array of technology devices and media. Communication delivery elapses in seconds, rather than hours and days.

Where does digital communication fall now particularly in the workplace? Studies point to the importance of non-verbal communication, as noted with Dr. Albert Mehrabian's conclusion that words account only for 7% of communication, and the remaining from other queues (non-verbal - 55% and vocal - 38%). (Blake, 2011) Email, online or social media channels lack non-verbal context, such as facial expressions or tonality. A growing challenge remains to effectively communicate in an increasing digital channel and lacking face to face access. Without non-verbal elements, virtual messages as text and email are unpredictably subject to individual interpretation and unforeseen reactions. Our best practices foster employee awareness and more positive outcomes with communication use.

Emerging technologies converge with communication channels faster than ever and affect every workplace and industry. New products redefine the speed, manner and the way communication happens. Increasingly, the emerging dominance of online channels challenge the traditional constructs of face to face conversations. Herein lays a challenge to harness new technology in social media, email and messaging, while trying to understand its use and effectiveness – on and off of the job. One might liken this juggling act as reading the instruction manual while trying to fly the airplane! Now is the time to document, communicate and enforce a user manual on technology etiquette and communications. As more businesses invest in technology, the ability to talk, work and interface with team members, employees or clients is increasingly digitized. Seemingly 'everyone' is online, as the statistics reveal more than 216.6 million US adults use email in 2013, and 78.4% of U.S. adult users send an email at least once monthly. (EMarketer, 2013)

A new frontier grows as personal tablets or smartphone use increases to view corporate messaging. The data shows no slowdown in the amount or frequency. New devices infiltrate consumer and corporate markets daily and increase content sharing tools. Many corporations now standard issue smartphones and/or tablets that include even more tools for 24/7 email and text enabled access. The omnipresence of devices and notifications drive more use in and out of the office, whether on the networks, through the corporate Internet or email server. As lines increasingly blur between 'off duty' and 'on duty' use, employers need to set guidelines for employees regarding corporate devices. Policies and training need to outline the approved use of social media channels as well, including corporate hashtags, Facebook posts and photo tagging on and off hours.

More businesses forgo desktop computers and face to face meetings in lieu of conferencing and tablets. Technology connects employees with devices utilizing corporate networks, Internet access, and conferencing tools. (Acxiom) With the virtualization of communications, businesses face financial decisions to automate more processes to online, virtual or digital avenues. From healthcare to non-profit industries, technology decisions increasingly influence more process automation and communication channels. Further still, nearly every industry reveals decreasing face-time servicing channels and more automated tools. Consider the supermarket's "Self Service Checkout Kiosk", the library's self-service book return or the bank's automated teller machine and digital check processing. Etiquette policies need to address new channels without compromising service and relationships standards. Our best practices recommend an annual survey to assess customer, client and patient satisfaction and quality control in these channels.

Our client experiences reveal a startling risk with the vast amount of employees untrained in file management, basic software etiquette, data risks, and device use. As alternative channels emerge, users access corporate email on multiple devices and often without password protection. The ability to download corporate data to an unsecured device challenges data confidentiality, compliance and security regulations. Since many devices offer a download or 'save as' feature, policy consideration and user discretion is needed in training policies as well. Whether your company manages clients, patients, donors, members, customers, vendors or contractors, each of these constituencies represent data to protect and potential distribution threats in technology usage. Your technical etiquette policies need to address the omnipresence of devices and impact to governance, access and security. Our client best practices include etiquette considerations for file management and distribution practices to safeguard company data and establish consistent file management, security and storage practices.

The Foundation of Technology Etiquette

Constant notification beeps and ringtones distract the most casual of conversations and interrupt the most formal of presentations. As a result, employees often read the screen instead of each other's faces. Every organization needs to detail the acceptable use of technology in every department and for every employee. While the Sales, Marketing and Business Development teams may approve tweets during meetings, the executive or operations teams may deem this unacceptable, disruptive or even dangerous. Technology etiquette standards need to define the value and need for device use and access. Additionally the policies need to also address the style and content of such use. A baseline standard should be set for professionalism in all correspondence, voice-mail, meetings, social media and other channels.

Technology etiquette policies apply to employees, contractors and volunteers and every age group. By developing a policy, organizations can define a consistent benchmark for office culture and productivity. With mixed demographics of office teams, stark differences exist to define 'accepted' use of technology. While multi-tasking is recognized as a badge of efficiency in some circles, this may not translate in other teams, such as executive or management levels. To enforce organizational effectiveness, organizations need to set a standard – now.

Our client examples find mixed adoption of technology and acceptable behaviors with use and access. Without a policy, employee satisfaction ratings often point to morale, productivity or impacts due to technology use. A corporate standard helps to mediate the tension between an intern's tweeting habit and a manager's request to meet in person. Your head buried in a Smartphone may not translate as courteous or professional during the CEO's board presentation. Our client experiences identified gaps attributable to technology etiquette: whether a clinical staff missed a critical patient update while checking messages – or a financial officer missed a pricing change while tweeting during the call. As this technology's use grows, it's time to reconsider technology etiquette without compromising efficiency or employee access to information. We recommend a standard be adopted that is consistent to existing communication channels, relevant to your audiences and acceptable to employees. Internal focus groups, surveys or discussions can help define acceptable uses.

Core Elements of Technology Etiquette

Below are key components of enforceable technology etiquette plans:

- ✓ Define what, how and when to use devices.
- ✓ Train every single employee in technology etiquette.
- ✓ Never tweet, answer a phone or text during an interview.
- ✓ Always be professional and never curse in any channel. If you can't send the message to the CEO or your grandmother, rewrite or delete.
- ✓ Train employees to reread messages and how to use "Forward", "Share" and "Send".
- ✓ Ensure that device use does not distract or compete with conversation, a presenter, client (customer/patient), interviewer, emergency staff or supervisor.
- ✓ Remove headphones, buds, or Bluetooth pieces, unless needed i.e. training, servicing, conferencing, safety, etc.
- ✓ Gaming is never professionally acceptable in a meeting, unless employed in such an industry or approved for use by administration or moderator at break or defined period.
- ✓ Mute devices in common areas, i.e. restrooms, cafes, cubicles, conference rooms, etc. and test the "mute" functionality prior to a call or webinar.
- ✓ Reread every message, tweet, post or email before sending.
- ✓ Avoid personal photo uploads, "selfies" or links to corporate social media sites, posts, hashtags or profile set-up, or on your desk.

Define rules for device use during a meeting such as:
- *Promotional, sales, marketing and publicity use*: generate buzz or communicating updates
- *Working meeting*: all attendees agree to maximize the working session of the meeting and use devices.
- *Customer service, Relationship and business development*: connect or service with effective and immediate response, respond to customer.
- *Sales, Servicing, Care, Operations, Escalation needs*: addressing patient, customer, client, manager, executive, safety/ security or timely needs.
- *Research Need*: as approved by the speaker or decorum.
- *Other Priorities*: as approved by the Moderator or Speaker.

CHAPTER II

Messaging Etiquette

Email - Overview

Your technology etiquette polices must address messaging in all formats, from email to text messaging. Since the first message sent in 1971, text and email volume continues to explode with increasing personal and corporate use on multiple devices. More than one in four email users access email on a smartphone, compared to 69% from a computer, and 5% on a tablet. (LiveIntent, 2013) Email messages, responses and newsletters need to be brief, as users average 51 seconds per email (Email V7 Usability, 2010). Best practices include brief email responses and without personal or proprietary information. Software like Microsoft Outlook and Google Gmail offers tools to manage conversation threads containing multiple email responses to the same subject. Policies need to enforce that email senders extend the same professional courtesies as in face to face meetings. Employees should use other forums to resolve, communicate or debate issues instead of messaging. Consider each of the messaging elements described below for your etiquette policy.

Email Responsiveness

Courtesy, customer response and servicing expectations should be specified for messaging etiquette. Any message requires a prompt response, whether email or text. Our client standards consider one to two working days a reasonable standard, but vary based on job duties and needs. If a person is out of the office for the day or longer, an auto-response email is recommended. This notification should be triggered from the email receipt and clearly define a contact person, telephone number and email address. Email providers offer an "Out of the Office Assistant" or "Automatic Replies" to assist with internal and an external response set-up. This standard also applies to those industry employees required to carry a beeper or text messaging service.

Best Practices: Email Content

Before computers, all corporate correspondence prints on company letterhead. Every letter displays consistency in color, elements and style. The company controls the communication presentation, structure and content with formality. Each letter includes a greeting, salutation, body and ending signature, typist initials and optional enclosure and copy notifications. In a comparable sense, the email message requires the same elements to maintain a professional standard of communication and brand representation.

Figure: Letter vs. Email Components

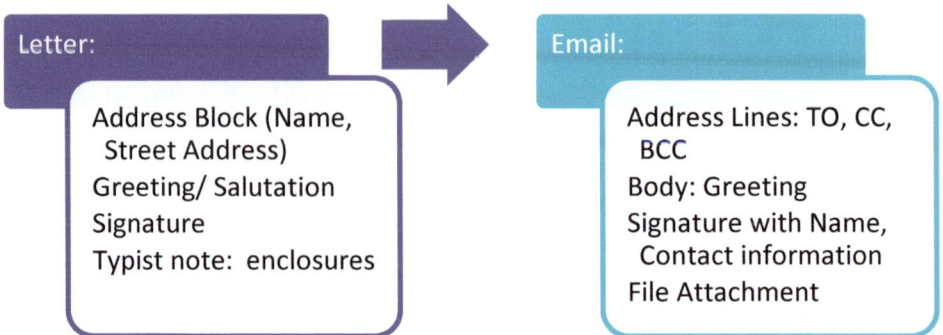

Email messages offer parallel structure to letter writing, as both should adhere to basic grammar and spelling rules. Regardless of the online delivery, the message replicates the formality of letter structure, including a salutation or greeting and an ending sign-off. The immediacy of delivery response should not relax the professionalism of the message or response. Emoticons (i.e. 'smiley faces') and clipart can detract from professional standards and are not encouraged. The structure of the email generally includes full sentences with these guidelines:

- Capitalize the first word of each sentence.
- Write in complete sentences with a subject and verb.
- Punctuate sentences.

Your etiquette policy needs to address email messaging as an employee framework for design, content and addressing. Email differs from letter writing or printed correspondence, as created in a word processing program like Microsoft Word or Google Docs. As culled from our clients' best practices, an email message should be brief, concise, and targeted to one topic. No justification is substantiated to use cursing, slanderous or offensive language in any online, text messaging or email communication. The risk lies in the uncontrollability of the message once sent. ANY message (email, text, comment, tweet, post) can be shared, forwarded or blind carbon –copied to any person with an email address, internal or external. A user can never assume the email is not read or accessed by another person in or out of the company. All messaging is subject to corporate guidelines, state and federal law, including sexual harassment.

Best Practices: Email Addressing – a Lost Art?

Email message structure mirrors that of a letter. To write a letter, the author enters the recipient's name and address in the upper corner, body text in the center, and ends with a salutation and distribution list(s). Similarly, composing an email message mirrors the same needs: *who, what, where* and *who else*. Each email message requires valid email addresses and a subject line.

Best practices include:

Email:	Tool:	Best practices:
TO:	**To line** - a list of the primary recipients to receive the email, and displays email addresses in this field.	✓ Target required employees. ✓ Minimize the number in the TO: line.
FROM:	**From Line** – displays the email address of the sender.	✓ Always display a person or known corporate figure. ✓ Display company name. ✓ Avoid use of numbers or characters.
CC:	**Carbon Copy Line** – a list of secondary recipients to receive a copy of the email, and displays email addresses in this field.	✓ Limit over-use. ✓ Avoid blanket "FYI" copies to a department, team or company distribution group.
BCC:	**Blind Carbon Copy Line** – a list of recipient(s) to receive the email, but the email address and name are only visible to the sender ('blind' to all others on the email).	✓ Limit the use of this field to support transparent and open communication lines culturally. ✓ Acceptable to use for marketing, sales and business development external "seeding" to protect email identities.
SUBJECT:	**Subject line** – a short title of the email.	✓ Limit Subject line text to 25 – 50 characters. ✓ Avoid ALL CAPS, numbers in the Subject line.

When responding to an email, many email programs add a reference to the email's subject line and indicates the type of messaging response. Remind employees to not remove these:

- RE: Reply or Reply to All
- FW: Forward

Email can be forwarded, printed, copied and distributed – without any knowledge or control by the user. Forwarding of private email violates copyright law and etiquette standards. Best practices include the following uses of the RE: and the FW: fields:

Email:	Tool:	Best practices:
RE:	*Reply or Reply to All Lines* – return a response email to the sender or all of the recipients who display on the TO: and CC: lines.	✓ Manage the *Reply* and *Reply to All* tools. All employees should discretionally use the "reply to all" command. ✓ Never reply all to a company distribution or department wide communication, e.g. Human Resources, Sales, Legal, etc.
FW:	*Forward* –send a message to recipients not originally on the email distribution, which includes attachments.	✓ Never forward unsolicited email. ✓ Always review the recipient list and body text prior to forwarding. ✓ Never forward confidential, sensitive or restricted email without checking recipients, encryption needs, etc.
BODY:	Email Text Body – compose the email content.	✓ Clear, brief and less than 250 words total. ✓ Use Web friendly fonts: *Arial, Verdana, Georgia* and *Times New Roman*. ✓ Use a third party image tool to compress graphic size. ✓ Limit formatting to inline styles or bullets. ✓ Start a new email with a short summary.

Design options:

Because of email's explosive growth, technology etiquette policy needs to define messaging design standards for employees. Our client experiences find that employee's email inbox and device messaging folders clutter with ineffectively written and excessively stored messages. To be effective, each email should contain a single topic related to the Outlook Subject. This standard fosters easy search functionality and more effective recipient follow-up. Users need to compose a new email or 'thread' if a new topic emerges in the conversation and never change a "Subject" line once submitted.

Remind employees to keep email message content as short and factual, with a professionally 'neutral' tone. Remember, recipient(s) cannot read tonality, sarcasm or intent. Stay on point, and consider alternative, face to face communication for performance or discipline issues. Every corporate email and text message is required by State and Federal laws to comply with Sexual Harassment and Human Resource law. *It's the law.*

Email design requires concise body text and a short, specific subject defined. As screens shrink in size, more users read email on a smaller screen, such as tablets and smartphones. No stationery templates should be used in any message, as this is unreadable on many smartphone screens. Ignore formatting and graphic design tools in email software, and use text. The best practices include no background color scheme, even if brand focused. Avoid pictures, quotes and personalized styles in signatures, even the logo. Server technology also can prevent object content download at the signature level and blocks the message display.
- Formality:
    - No txt-ing in email. Spell-out abbreviations.
    - Limit jokes or sarcasm. NEVER curse.
- Content:
    - Avoid all capital letters.
    - Avoid emoticons.
    - Minimize use of jargon.
- Length:
    - Avoid long, emotional email messaging.
    - Avoid personal related email distribution.

Your technology policy needs to address access to personal devices on corporate messaging tools. Additional considerations should identify if and when personal email access is acceptable at work, such as *Yahoo, Google, Comcast,* etc. Both personal messaging and use of devices pose challenges to corporate compliance and network security standards. Our client experience finds increased virus and malware risks through such systems, higher employer exposure to security risks and decreased productivity. Many corporations now restrict access to personal or consumer based email systems on the job. Often human resource and information protocols limit employee access and use to personal use of devices or technology and especially during office hours. Etiquette policies should outline any employee penalties or termination risks with repeated violations or misuse.

Three technology issues may block or impede the view of email design elements in our client experiences across industries:

1. Newer server technology prompts a manual download of any objects, such as picture graphics in email messages.
2. Email browser settings may restrict the presentation of fonts or non-text based formatting if HTML (hypertext markup language) is not selected.
3. Avoid the use of themes or stationery in email design as this blocks text messaging display on smaller device screens, such as a smartphone or tablet.

Alternative email design solutions include:
- Add an <alt> text for images to display an alternative text line if the server suspends the graphic display.
- Use the Clipboard function (Cut/Copy/ Paste) only in HTML email formatting, as the source code does not display predictably.
- Use the *Insert* tab instead to add an object if needed, to an email message. Remember, some devices or servers may impede or block the object display and/or download.
- Design for the Preview pane with key information displaying in the top 2 – 4 inches or 400 – 600 pixels wide of the message.
- Use a minimum of twelve (12) or fourteen (14) point font size, black font color and no fill to enhance readability.

To summarize, our shared best practices include:

Text	Graphics	Design
Brief & Factual	Minimal graphics, theme	Signature only
No emoticons	or stationery in messaging	NO Themes
Use 14 points for body text	Logo only	Design <600 pixels wide to
Spell check	Low resolution	fit screen

File Attachment protocols:

Your company technology standards need to define guidelines for file attachments and document uploads. We find many employees overuse attachments and uploads to distribute files. Such practices stress email server capacity and storage limits, while exposing potential areas of network security risk. Training employees on proper file management, download and upload practices, and use of online and shared drives, can lessen the overall system hardware costs of storage and mistakes. Main policy components should address file size, content and audience.

Size: Most email and social media programs support multiple file attachments or photo uploads for distribution. Every recipient on the message receives a copy of the file(s) attached, which includes the *To, Carbon Copy* and the *Blind Carbon Copy* recipients. But many email servers restrict the size of each message and all attachments to ten megabytes or less. Regular inbox clean-up and archiving is recommended, as all files count toward storage limits. Email etiquette suggests restricting large file attachment distribution to avoid negatively impacting the recipient's storage. Text or SMS messages should follow the same protocols as email.

Content: Separate file attachments should be managed based on the audience, size and content. The best practices below offer alternatives to consider: 1) minimize message size, 2) preserve formatting or 3) restrict editing. Tools such as file links and read only file formats protect sensitive, proprietary and confidential information. Avoid clicking on Spam, virus or malware links and especially any unknown executable (*exe) file.

Our clients' best practices for file attachments, downloads or uploads include:

Alternative	Best Practices:
Monitor overall message size.	Attachments and messages should be less than 10 MB (megabytes) for email distribution. Use share or link features.
Add a note to the Subject Line if attaching larger files.	Type: "Warning: Large File Attachments in Subject".
Use compression tools to reduce file attachment size(s).	Use WinZip or Picture tools to compress images. Maintain a maximum object width of 600 pixels for online distribution.
Attach a hyperlink or paste a link to a shared or network source.	An embedded or pasted link to a file allows the user to open and edit the content and requires appropriate clearance and security access to the content. ** *Caution*: send only to a trusted source and/or internal resource. ** Never open an executable file (*.exe) as this often derives from a virus, malware or suspicious source.
Attach a read-only file format or pasted picture (or bitmap).	Use a *Portable Document Format* (PDF) or *Bitmap* (BMP) picture file to prevent file editing, but allows recipient(s) to read and print.
Use only professional file attachments in download or upload processes.	Avoid use of personal images or documents on a corporate network, in file management use, email attachments, file storage, linking, or social media use.

Audience: Every employee requires training on file management, Windows or Google Drive and data management best practices. Our client experience find startling gaps in employees' lack of training and understanding of file sharing, storing and distribution tools. Our client experiences reveal data breaches, file misuse and security lapses on every corporate level and in every industry. Security risks exist with every employee to safeguard legally protected data, such as HIPPA patient medical records, customer financial statements, student records or the company's trade secrets. The powerful ability for any employee to share, send, download and distribute exists in every smartphone as well as the vast array of corporate tools at their disposal.

Our best practices recommend the etiquette policy include training on external and external distribution of files. File attachments and email messages require risk management and protection of sensitive data. Compliance and legal rules apply to file attachments and govern the security and management of all data. All email, text and social media messages, electronic transmissions and attachments must follow established procedures and regulations governing the content, and safeguard the company's property and confidentiality. In some cases, file attachments and/or email messages require encryption, or additional coding and security keys, to protect the data. As an example, healthcare employees must not email patient medical record numbers without encryption and proper adherence to HIPPA, federal and state regulations.

All employees need to take precautions to *check, assess,* and *manage* risk associated with file distribution. Personal files, including photos, should not be stored on a corporate issued device, drive or social media site. If a user saves or downloads an attached corporate file to a network location, public computer or portable device, this file must be permanently deleted. Users should check the files stored in the local *Documents>Download* folder, or remove files downloaded from the Internet or external drive from the computer. All Internet browsers also provide a tool to delete the *history*, or cached pages upon exit. With embedded storage, Clipboard's *Paste Special* and *Links* tools require assessments of any distribution risks. Users need to check every cell, sheet, page, and formula for sensitivity and access to source files. Your etiquette policy needs to detail employee requirements for entry, file management and distribution protocols.

Best practices for File Attachments:

Internal file attachments	External file attachments
Use workbook links and object pasting if a trusted resource or signed confidentiality agreement.	Require a review for confidential and sensitive message contact and file attachments.
Use a read-only file format to display sensitive or proprietary information, restrict cells, and block editing.	Never forward a detailed, internal email response to an outside contact.
Send a link to a cloud or network file location instead of attaching large files.	Create a new email with the appropriate response, including a status update, date and owner.
Protect the data and/or the file with a password (safeguard).	Encrypt sensitive or protected data.
Never attach, upload or download personal files on corporate devices.	Avoid embedded documents, spreadsheets or prersentations with confidential or proprietary data.

The technology etiquette policy should document a checklist for employees to check file data, including:
- Check for internal or sensitive information.
- Check every sheet or page for data or links.
- Understand the *Save/ Send* feature of file attachments that contain sensitive, compliant or mandated data.
- Know encryption policies, i.e. HIPPA, Financial reports.
- Click through *Clipboard Paste* links of Excel workbooks, PowerPoint presentations or Word documents.
- Check every formula, embedded table and *Paste Values*.
- Alert employees to ways to protect their files, including:
    - Paste Special as Picture or Bitmap
    - *Read only document* format for external distribution, such as *Adobe PDF* (Portable Document Format) *File Type* or *XPS* (Extensible Paper Specifications) File
- Enabling password protection of document.

Signatures

Every email requires a signature, or display of the sender's contact information at the bottom of the email. Software program such as Microsoft Outlook and Google's Gmail provides an automated tool for *Signature*. Avoid quotes, inspiration messages or graphics other than an approved use of the corporate logo. The signature use should be for set for use in *Replies* and *Forwards* messaging. Some corporations establish a brand standard or communication protocol governing employee signatures. This procedure standardizes a consistent employee contact profile and specific font size, font color and formatting guidelines. In the absence of a formal policy, the best practice requires the employee set-up an internal and an external signature with appropriate contact information and escalation data.

Signature data requires the following (as applicable):

- Name
- Title/Position
- Company Name
- Address
- Telephone Number
- Email Address/Beeper
- Escalation contact data
- Mail Stop

In summary, email messaging represents one of the fastest growing, most prevalent means of communication in business. Our client experiences benchmark an etiquette standard to consider in the email design, addressing, content and inclusion of file attachments. As a communication channel, any messaging follows the same standards as offline channels and requires sensitivity to employee policies. The immediacy of email delivery requires additional sensitivity to email tonality and wording, as well as the responses' confidentiality and distribution. Our best practices identify protocols to consider for a company –wide policy on the proper email usage on and off hours. The most effective solution includes defining, training and enforcing a consistent offline and online communication standard to internal and external employees, vendors and contractors on all devices.

Using Text Messaging

In addition to email, a similarly instantaneous channel emerges to communicate via tablet or smartphone: the *text message*. Since the first message from a computer to a phone by Neil Papworth in 1992, text messaging continues to dominate communications with its short lined capture over a phone network (Beal, 2013) Forrester Research summarized that six billion messages communicate daily in the United States, which adds up to 2.2 trillion annually. (Grady, 2012) As social media and app usage grows, messaging continues to outpace the number of phone calls received in nearly every age group. The growing use of messaging remains an efficiency tool and a way to streamline processing and begs for consideration of a corporate etiquette policy. Industry polices vary on the accessibility, usage and integration of text messaging in the workplace, and require situation assessment, monitoring and rules. (Halverson, 2013) Our best practice recommends the creation of a corporate policy on text messaging frequency, response times, content and audience approved for corporate text messaging. Newer technology allows messages to display once and then disappear, and also requires etiquette standards. Spelling and grammar rules apply as needed, as do human resource policies on employee communications and corporate brand use.

Best Practices for Text Messaging and Social App:
Personal
- Establish protocols for personal messaging on corporate devices, including text, Snapchat, Kik and other apps.
- Determine who, how, when and where messaging occurs.
- Outline times and places acceptable for personal messaging.
- Avoid cursing or inappropriate language in email, messaging, corporate hashtags or posts-- ever.
- Avoid personal photo uploads or "selfies" to corporate sites.
- Use a personal email address when using social media.

Corporate
- Create a brand standard for text messaging template(s).
- Determine who, how, when and where messaging occurs.
- Establish monitoring processes, and reports for compliance.
- Publish a brand standard on usage and access and communicate to <u>all employees</u>.
- Outline acceptable usage and access for messaging in policies, operations and services on corporate devices.

CHAPTER III

Social Media

Social Media & Etiquette

As a defacto corporate standard exists today, most employers deploy a web site presence and email address system to compete in this global economy. Notwithstanding the growth of web site content and email messaging, social media continues to also grow as a corporate tool. In fact, social media represents one of the most electrifying enterprise channels in industry today. This online community serves not only as an emerging digital marketing strategy, but as a communication channel, commerce, networking, operational, sales, servicing and relationship building strategy. Social media tactics complement existing brand strategies in an increasingly diverse marketing mix.

However, social media's viral nature is instantaneous and global. This poses networking, security and publicity implications for your company, your brand and your employees. As with every communication channel, organizations need to develop corporate etiquette standards for social media. Organizations need to analyze social media's benefits and risks and formulate appropriate planning. Employers need to define the approved employee use and access to social media channels, and develop acceptable technology etiquette practices. As the strategy unfolds, your employees needs to understand, train and satisfy corporate guidelines for technology etiquette. Policies help to maintain a professional presence in the marketplace for sales, operational servicing, and building relationships for all employees.

The etiquette manual serves to educate employees on expectations and protects the corporate image. With more Internet enabled devices, employers' policies should define employees' assess and use of social media channels in personal and professional venues. With accessibility from any internet enabled device, any employee can gain instant, worldwide notoriety with a single tweet. While social medial channels deliver cross organizational and multi -functional value, every post or tweet holds <u>immediate</u> global reach. The level of penetration and publicity buzz is unparalleled in speed and lack of controls.

The instantaneous delivery of social media requires the availability of resources to manage editorial content. Corporations face exposure 24 hours a day to employees, customers and the public's use and access to your social media sites. From photo tags to file links, each social media site offers an instant ability to communicate and lacks a "STOP" button. No corporate controls exist to prevent negative, malicious or wrong content to display or link. Create a plan to manage brand risk, customer complaints or employee misuse swiftly. For maximum effectiveness, etiquette protocols must define a professional standard that applies to employees, whether accessing a corporate or personal device. Your company reaps enriching publicity, broadened marketing reach, and brand value, but needs to minimize risks. The company can utilize existing system protocols to limit access to specific online sites and block unsolicited email notifications from the email servers.

Best Practices for Social Media Etiquette Standards:

Your etiquette policy should address employee usage and employee access in every site used in corporate marketing, i.e. *Facebook*, *LinkedIn* and *Twitter*. Recommendations include:

✓ Every employee needs to understand and train in the acceptable use of email, online use and social media access, including tags, posts, photo uploads and hashtag use.
✓ Dedicate a full-time resource to create content, edit, service, monitor and analyze results.
✓ Maintain valuable, fresh and interactive social media content.
✓ Identify the right social media site and marketing mix for your company, brand and mission.
✓ Survey constituents, internal employees, vendors, customers and partners to determine social media need and appeal.
✓ Create online and social media channels as integrated channels. Do not create an isolated Facebook site or launch a Twitter site without inter-office dialogue or employee feedback.
✓ Keep the social media tags simple and brand related, e.g. #CompanyName.

As with each technology channel, employers need to outline policies on use, access and etiquette standards. An etiquette protocol should be created, communicated and trained upon for all corporate employees, vendors and constituents regarding social media. This ever- changing landscape reveals differing legal opinions, case law precedents and industry practices for employer and employee usage of social media. Risks exist to manage the approved employee access, usage and representation in any channel (i.e. offline and online).

Below are the key priorities and examples, as defined in our clients' roll-out of social media strategies and procedures:

Best Practices in Social Media:

Best Practice	Example / Scenario:
Define the social media sites acceptable to access on company time, if at all, and determine the timing, frequency and duration.	Permit use at lunch or break.
Define employees' use of the corporate domain, personal email address and corporate hashtag in their social media profiles, posts and updates.	Only tweet Marketing/Sales comments using the #CorpName.
Separate personal use from the corporate sites. No corporate email address is used in employee profiles.	Create a free personal email to use in your profile or account set-up.
Identify the approved uses of the corporate logo, links, trademark content or proprietary information in social media channels.	Avoid posting links to corporate web site from personal tweet or post.
Create a business page or profile to update, network, and brand and publish employee rules on posts, links, uploads or friend use.	Encourage employees to 'like' a corporate page. Prohibit managers from 'friending' direct reports.
Build a Social Media team to meet regularly to create and edit content.	Engage all departments. Publish weekly releases.
Create rich, valuable content that includes updates, photographs and news.	Create a media guide for social media. Create a weekly posting schedule with owners.
Identify the types of content allowed for each department to link, publish, post or use in social media channels or on corporate web site(s).	Encourage employees to link or post photos from corporate events, but in professional settings. Avoid restroom "selfies".

As with every channel, our best practices recommend the formation of a team to develop and launch a social media or website. This ensures consistency within the corporate culture and integrated approach to managing risk and reward. Ongoing oversight is needed to edit instantaneous and viral content and manage community response. When resourced and managed properly, social media offers a robust channel to generate positive publicity, awareness and cultivate new channels, including:

- Market new and existing products and services.
- Create buzz and publicity.
- Update customers, clients, prospects and stakeholders.
- Drive traffic to retail or online channels.
- Broaden brand and corporate awareness.
- Engage audiences with targeted and personalized content.
- Drive community building and interaction.
- Build value and communication.
- Build a new distribution and marketing channel.
- Service clients or customers through email driven channels.
- Drive customer revenue, retention and loyalty.

Organizations should analyze the channels' effectiveness for operational, monetary and marketing value and benchmark as part of the etiquette policy making process. Our clients' best practices set monthly performance metrics, including:

- *System traffic* - page hits, click-thrus, email opens.
- *Marketing effectiveness*- number of tweets /retweets, number of Facebook posts and likes, penetration of user conversion clicks.
- *Monetary profitability* – amount of sales or donations from channel links, number of referrals, leads and closings, amount of expenses (hardware, software, personnel, security, etc.)
- *Resourcing* – number of FTE (full time employees) dedicated to channel, number of hours allocated, contractor needs, etc.
- *Relationship building* – number of friends or connections; percentage of conversion to accounts or sales, number of customers sourced from social media; number of consecutive years of donating or sales.

Our Client Best Practices for Social Media, Technology Etiquette:

Facebook

Define employee rules for posting to corporate pages or liking content.
Assign an editor to manage the Facebook "wall", update profile, check and respond to posts, manage "likes" and approve posts.
Drive traffic to site with targeted emails, advertising and cross-links.
Publish a standard for employee personal usage of the corporate brand, logo, "likes", links, posts, uploads, tags or mentions on Facebook.
Publish an employee guideline to post or attach corporate files, photo tagging, attaching pictures, "selfies" and comments on corporate pages.

Twitter

Design employee standards for using company hashtag # and handle.
Restrict hashtag use to brand, promote, sell or inform.
Publish employee guidelines for corporate tweets, comments, retweets and photo sharing, particularly on personal accounts. No personal selfies!
Publish internal press releases or Intranet invitations for employee promotion of viral content and awareness building. Publish rules to use!
Identify approved marketing, sales, service and other promotion calendar items and communicate to internal and external constituents.
Create a media plan with frequent and value-added content.

LinkedIn

Encourage all employees to setup a profile for networking.
Create an "alumni" group for employees.
Use LinkedIn Profiles to vette new hires and recruits.
Require employees to set-up a free, personal email account for the LinkedIn profile.
Discourage use of corporate email address in account set-up.
Establish an Editorial Review board for corporate content.
Encourage management and executive staff to publish approved and brand friendly content in groups.
Recommend employees and vendors on LinkedIn.
Consider sales lead and advertising strategies.

CHAPTER IV

Remote Conferencing

As tele-commuting roles increase, so too does the need to set etiquette standards for virtual presenters and attendees too. Our client best practice experiences identify the following elements for an effective remote meeting, webinar or conference call. Increasing use of distance or remote meeting tools suggests a need to set etiquette standards and technology checks to ensure a professional meeting standard. A general rule of thumb for technology etiquette requires promptness always to initiate an online meeting, web based, teleconference or video conference or webinar. The virtualization of the meeting necessitates the moderator and speaker(s) on both ends of the technology test the equipment's accessibility and navigation prior to the meeting.

Employers and employees need to establish a professional benchmark and preserve etiquette for both the presenter and the audience in distractions, response and channel logistics. Distractions represent a challenge in and out of the office due to the omnipresent background noise, beeping devices and the pressures of 24 hour accessibility. Internal and external stimuli vary, but maintaining a professional environment is crucial for meeting efficacy. Remote employees may have to balance pets and children, while internal employees face garrulous cube-mates and candy jar crowd gatherings for noise distractions. To minimize background chatter, consider solutions – whether treats for the dogs, puzzles for the kids, or signs for the cubicle.

The second component addresses response based distractions. The speaker and audience should follow a decorum similar to a face to face meeting. An agenda is distributed prior to any meeting, indicating the call leader, discussion agenda or order of talking points, the telephone dial-in or web access instructions and password and special instructions. To begin any meeting, the organizer initiates greetings and introductions, agenda, and announcements. The chairperson or meeting organizer controls the 'floor' or grants control to one person speaking at a time. Our best practice calls for the moderator to announce the handling of questions and answers at the beginning of the call. Etiquette requires all attendees refrain from typing during the meeting and multi-tasking. To close a call, best practices include a recap of action items, follow-up points and closing salutation. The organizer is responsible to distribute minutes within a week of the held meeting (or sooner) for project or time sensitive requests.

The last component requires managing channel logistics. As previously discussed, the organizer and attendee needs to set-up, test and activate required audio visual and conferencing equipment. Your etiquette standard should require the organizer to open a conference line a few minutes prior to the official start of the meeting, efficiently close the line and stop the recording. Best practices include checking the following elements:

- o Meeting recording
- o Mute button and call waiting preferences
- o Handling/availability of question and answers (email, online, text based)
- o Activation for additional lines or channels (audio, video, web)

As tele-commuting roles increase, so too does the need to set etiquette standards for virtual attendees. Any meeting space or professional discussion commands a comfortable and professionally quiet environment to conduct business. Whether working remotely on the home sofa or sprawled in a cubicle with headphones, many employees face the daunting task of managing distractions. From noisy cubicle officemates to watercooler chatter, from barking dogs to Kuerig coffee making, from deliveries to vacationing children's play, from toilet flushes to inadvertent mute buttons during the "Candy Crush" high score; war stories abound for breaches in conference call protocols. The value of remote conferencing is the ability to view facial expressions and add context recipients' response while managing background distractions in a non-corporate environment.

Our best practice undeniably recommends that all employers create, communicate and train employees on technology etiquette expectations during in person or web based meetings, and enforce a level of professionalism always. A meeting is a meeting is a meeting, and should follow the same professional standards and courtesies whether conducted in person, on the web, in audio and video conferencing, in messaging or any other channel. Technology use or access should never compromise the value of another person, a relationship or the meeting's purpose. Balance is always recommended, in the use and access of device in an organization.

Below lists our meeting best practices for etiquette:

Managing distractions

Control background noise (pets, family).
Consider a white noise filter if you are a remote or virtual employee.
Use signs to signal 'off' times for deliveries or visits to the office, cube , etc. to minimize background noise.
No typing while unmuted as keystrokes magnify on the conference line.

Managing Response

Publish an agenda for every meeting.
Request specific time from the moderator chair to speak.
Never speak over another speaker.
Extend greetings and closings .
Set ground rules at the start of every meeting for device use,

Managing Channel Logistics

Setup and distribute the conference line access number, password and equipment *prior to the start of the meeting*.
Disable message beeps or audio notifications.
Test "Mute" button before meeting and bathroom breaks.

Managing Cultural Differences

Research language and cultural communications , particularly for international clients and native countries' business protocols and communication standards (i.e .hand gestures, idioms, gift giving, etc.)
Understand technology etiquette practices and share with teams prior to overseas meetings, calls or trips.
Schedule diversity and cultural training to understand speaking order, gestures, slang, or other communication elements that

Conferencing Checklist:

1. Check equipment's controls, including the speaker accessibility, volume and connection to other devices.
2. Understand mute options to enable and disable for both speaker(s) and audience members.
3. Determine the timing, protocols and messaging capability for speaker and audience: email, text, system based, call, conference, etc.
4. Check Internet connection, if required, for the actual meeting and/or file attachments.
5. Conduct a spot check for room 'dead zones' in video conferencing monitors, WIFI or network access if audience members are using mobile devices to conference.
6. Send links and meeting files at least one day prior to the meeting.
7. Check the System date/ time and synchronize for time zone variances as needed, e.g. all times are Eastern Standard Time, and allow audience members to adjust.
8. Rehearse video streaming and web based content on the presentation devices prior to the meeting, as slower machines may slow the display.
9. Remove transitions or animations for webinars and webcasting.
10. Request attendees remain muted if multi-tasking during a call or meeting, and to unmute to speak. Typing keys can add background noise distractions during a meeting or a call. Announce ground rules for attendee use and access of devices, including cell phones and pagers, prior to the start of the meeting.

CHAPTER V

Compliance

Compliance & Policy

All organizations need to balance the use of messaging and social media with your industry's legal, privacy and compliance standards. Human resources' employee orientation needs to include technology etiquette policy and training. Since all communication messages are corporate property, emerging channels like texting, email and social media require consideration. Employees represent the face of the company and the brand at events in person, in communications and virtually on any social media site. While the highest level of formality may be assumed in a letter or at the board table, your employee email messaging, hashtag, text message or posts may fall short of the corporate standard. The immediate delivery of messages challenges the most seasoned employers to conduct etiquette training before SEND or TWEET.

Employers typically provide computer hardware, software and access to the Internet, email and other channel. Whether internal or externally resourced, the company can monitor all incoming and outgoing communications within the network. Etiquette policies should address all messaging protocols and device access, whether server based (i.e. Outlook Exchange) or online based (i.e. Google Gmail). Corporate ownership entitles supervision and review of usage. Employees maintain few rights or guarantee of privacy in communications "on the job". (Tschabitscher, 2013)

External legislation affects employee rights regarding communications. On the federal level, the **Electronic Communications Privacy Act** generally allows companies to review email, (Justice, 2013) and generally "with their consent or in the ordinary course of business". This legislation defined electronic communication as *any transfer of signs, signals, writing, images, sounds, data or intelligence of any nature transmitted in whole or in part by a wire, radio, electromagnetic, photo electronic or photo-optical system* but excludes wire and oral communications. (Justice, 2013) Numerous state and federal lawsuits challenge employees' expectation of privacy and the employer's rights in online and offline channels. The employer owns all communications, including storage, access, surveillance and control of all email and online communications. With employment contracts or hiring, most employees relinquish control and privacy to their employers. This consent applies to any corporate telephone, mobile phone, computer, laptop, tablet or network. Internal corporate policy potentially restricts employee usage of any and all communications and channels to corporate use only and with employee consent. (Mukerji, 2013)

Employers' scope may extend beyond email messaging and corporate based communications. Now an employee's words, actions and behaviors on personal devices or "off-hours" may pose risk in online channels and be subject to corporate policies and litigation. Recent headlines point to employee misuse or violation of corporate policies due to Internet use, social media posts, and online event picture shares. The employees' verbal, nonverbal and printed communications count as corporate representation. Some companies take adverse action, even termination if an employee uses the corporate email address, logo, corporate name or hashtag negatively. Employees are recommended to use a secondary email address, and not the corporate email address in social media registrations or profile set-up. Employees may face penalties or human resource violations if personal usage violates corporate policies. Employers need to establish a sign-off for new hire orientation and existing employee training on social media usage and corporate representation in social media accounts. (Ballman, 2012) While social media networking is a highly useful channel, organizations need to create and communicate expectations for employees.

Etiquette protocols need to address technology access and control beyond the corporate network or internally issued laptops, phones or other devices. Virtual private networks, web access and other applications allow users to access business communications from outside of the company walls, including email, text messaging, network programs and databases. Increasingly, online based solutions and cloud technology allow users to access workspaces on any device. While security and firewall changes adapt to changing technology, employees increasingly rely on personal equipment and often without dependence on network security or systems for access. This poses a challenge to enforcing a secure, consistent and appropriate use of technology on corporate and personal devices.

As representatives of the company and its brand, the employee's technical footprint can travel quicker and more freely than ever before. Each organization needs to understand their target audience and the implications of social media and messaging channels. Policies need to define the acceptable use of photograph uploads, links, photo tagging, GPS location mapping and other online components in the etiquette policy and training. Each target audience or participant requires consideration of permission, media releases and sign-off, particularly with children or any protected constituent group. Additionally data intelligence, contract terms and patent related terms require protection in confidentiality and distribution.

Federal Law

Underscoring etiquette is the legal obligation of email communications, particularly in the marketing and solicitation avenues. The United States' federal government legislated rules for using email channel legally, as defined in the "**Controlling the Assault of Non Solicited Pornography and Marketing Act**" or know as CAN-SPAM Act and Canada's "**Personal Information Protection and Electronic Documents Act**" (PIPEDA). Email marketing requires email and online solicitations include the following elements for direct unsolicited email, including:

- Link to the company website, Phone number and email address.
- Identify the company clearly in the header.
- Keep the subject line clear and honest.
- Include a link to unsubscribe at no cost, maintained in a database, and take action within ten (10) days.
- Protect email addresses that unsubscribe.
- Include the company's postal address in email messages.

In summary, employees' use and access of technology requires compliance with all corporate policies for technical servicing, human resource, employee relations and brand marketing standards. Employers and employees must also adhere to local, state, federal and international guidelines as dictated in the states, territories and countries of their business. This manual outlines these considerations at a high level, but recommends specific guidance from internal advisors. Challenges exist for employer and employee to balance technology's value as a marketing, servicing and communication channel, while preserving the brand, culture and reputation of the company. Our best practices recommend defining etiquette in compliant, safe and legal use of technology for personal and professional devices and for alternative channels.

Conclusion

Communications continues to evolve in business. Every industry faces the challenge to invest in technology, whether hardware or software, laptop or computer, tablet or phone, pager or fax machine. Every employer assesses the need and financial return of technology for employees' access and use, and the correlates some gain to productivity, efficiency, profitability and satisfaction of customers (patients or clients) and employees. But employees face the pressures of 24x7 accessibility on personal and professional devices. Instantly gratifying, the sneak peak at the beep or message notification tempts every user and their sense of etiquette to respond. Undoubtedly, communication has transformed from the days of the Pony Express and letters, to instant messages, tweets and video conferencing.

Balancing emerging technology challenges the most seasoned, multi-tasking, globally networked response teams. An established etiquette protocol builds a consistent framework for employee and employer to harness technology. The implementation of these standards sustains a level of professional expectations and behavior. With communication and training, every employee better develops skills and behaviors to use the technology effectively and safely. Our client results show improved employee relations, organizational efficiencies, corporate morale and productivity with such established policies.

This book defines key technology etiquette components for organizations. Our best practices result from thousands of hours with healthcare, financial, government, municipal, non-profit, retail, and sole proprietor clients. As technology evolves, our breakthrough recommendations satiate a corporate need to set a professionally acceptable baseline for employee etiquette standards. Within the existing brand framework, employers gain industry norms for you, your employees' and customers' benefit. This book addresses the most critical etiquette components most impactful to the company's bottom line, organizational effectiveness and technological adaptation. This "411" request calls each of us to lift up those heads and balance those beeps.

Bibliography:

(2012, December). Retrieved December 1, 2013, from eMarketer: http://www.emarketer.com/Article/Email-Users-Reach-iPad/1009667

Acxiom. (n.d.). *"Email Marketing and Mobile Devices: A Survey of Consumer Habits and Perceptions"*. Retrieved November 13, 2013, from Email Stat Center.com: http://emailstatcenter.com/Usage.html

Ballman, D. (2012, December 9). *9 Ways Your Employer Can Legally Spy on You*. Retrieved August 10, 2013, from AOL Jobs: http://jobs.aol.com/articles/2012/12/09/employer-spy-workers-legally-snoop/

Beal, V. (2013, February 26). *Text Messaging and Online Chat Abbreviations*. Retrieved November 4, 2013, from Webopedia - Everything you need to know is right here: http://www.webopedia.com/quick_ref/textmessageabbreviations.asp

Blake. (2011, August). *How Much of Communication is Really Nonverbal*. Retrieved December 1, 2013, from The NonVerbal Group: http://www.nonverbalgroup.com/2011/08/how-much-of-communication-is-really-nonverbal/

Discovery Training Services. (2013). *2013 Etiquette Survey Results*. Wallingford, CT: DTS.

Edition, C. E.-C. (2009). *Merriam - Webster, An Excyclopedia Brittanica Company*. (W. C. Ltd., Editor, & Harper Collins Publishers 1998, 2000, 2003, 2005, 2006, 2007, 2009) Retrieved December 2, 2013, from www.m-w.com: http://dictionary.reference.com/browse/communication

eMarketer. (2013, March 4). *With Mature US Online Population, Small Gains for Email, Search Usage*. New York: US Internet Users 2013: Solid, Saturated Market for Web, Search and Email.

Flynn, N. F. (1998). *Writing Effective Email: Crisp 50 Minute Book*. NY: Crisp Publications.

Grady, M. O. (2012, June 19). *SMS Usage Remains Strong in the US: 6 Billion SMS Messages are Sent Each Day*. Retrieved March 13, 2014, from Forrester Research & Data: http://blogs.forrester.com/michael_ogrady/12-06-19-sms_usage_remains_strong_in_the_us_6_billion_sms_messages_are_sent_each_day

Halverson, C. (2013, February 1). *Go to When I Work*. Retrieved June 30, 2013, from When I Work: http://wheniwork.com/texting-in-the-workplace-establishing-a-company-policy/

Justice, U. D. (2013, July 30). *U.S. Department of Justice, Office of Justice Programs*. Retrieved December 3, 2013, from Privacy & Civil Liberties: Federal Statues: http://it.ojp.gov/default.aspx?area=privacy&page=1285

LiveIntent. (2013). *Opens by device Jan 2012 vs Jan 2013*. Retrieved December 1, 2013, from EmailMonday.com: http://www.emailmonday.com/mobile-email-usage-statistics

Mukerji, A. (2013, May 2). *"Is It Legal to Read Employees' Email?* Retrieved November 3, 2013, from The FindLaw Small Business Law Blog: http://blogs.findlaw.com/free_enterprise/2013/05/is-it-legal-to-read-employees-email.html

Online Etymology Dictionary - Communication. (2013). Retrieved 12 2, 2013, from Online Etymology Dictionary: http://www.etymonline.com/index.php?allowed_in_frame=0&search=communication&searchmode=none

Thank you to the many who supported this publishing effort, including the Mansfield family and Darlene Bailey.

www.ingramcontent.com/pod-product-compliance
Lightning Source LLC
Chambersburg PA
CBHW041144180526
45159CB00002BB/731